Bees to Baleens

The Rhyme & The Rhythm

OF LIVING THINGS

To: Kingsway Preparatory School Best Wishes! Beverly J. Hudson Oct. 7, 2018

FIRST EDITION

Poems & Illustrations By Beverly J. Hudson

Editor: Marjorie Hammons

NETFA Educational Publications
National City, CA

For Delise, who stamped
these poems "child approved,"
and to animal, art and poetry
lovers everywhere.

BJH

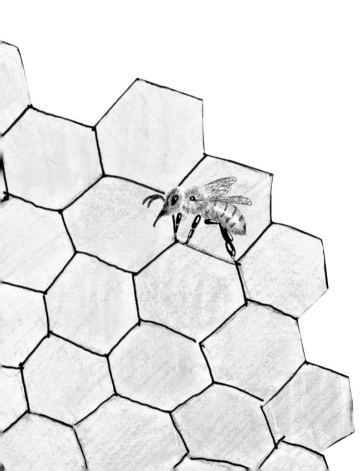

Mz. Bee

I'm busy buzzing all around
In my black and yellow gown.

I make the smoothest sweetest treat
And seal it up all nice and neat.

The flavors that my treats come in
Depend on the blossoms I've been in.

Apple, orange, cherry or plum
Just be sure to get you some.

4

Lady Butterfly

In your graceful mosaic gown

Come visit my garden

Where sweet nectar

May be found

Magnificent Mariposa

Floating in the air

Display your majestic beauty

For all the world to share

Papillion

Lady Bug

Lady bug, lady bug

In your red and black

Polka dot dress

When you come to the garden party,

You always look your best.

You rid the garden of pests

Like aphids and their kind.

And you never seem to make a mess,

So you're welcome anytime!

Grasshopper

Green, gangly, quick

Powerful back legs

Hopping in the tall green grass

Insect

Snail

I'm a snail
With a portable shell.
Well, actually it's my home.

And it goes with me
Over land and sea
Or wherever I may roam.

People talk behind my back;
They call me lazy and slow.

Well, just let them attach
Their homes to their backs
And see how far they'll go!

Spider

Spiders are cold-blooded arachnids.

They have eight legs in all.

Most weave webs in airy places,

Some lurk in dark, dank halls.

Some burrow holes into the ground

To wait upon their prey,

Others hunt near the water's edge

And this is where they stay.

And should an unfortunate insect

Get caught in one of their traps,

They drink their vital juices

Sip, Sip, Zap!

Scorpion

Scorpion, scorpion,

Where have you been?

Hiding in the rocks

'til the hot day's end.

Scorpion, scorpion,

What do you do then?

I hunt for insects all night long

'til another day begins.

M is for Mollusks

Mollusks are soft bodied animals
Protected by their shells,

Like oysters and clams
And slimy, sluggy snails.

Mussels huddle in groups
Anchored to their spots.

Limpets go it alone
Inching along on the rocks.

Most feed on algae
And other plant stuff,

But the Dog Whelk preys on barnacles
And other mollusks.

Starfish

Rose colored starfish
I'm glad we're both alive.

Hop right up here on this big sea rock
And give your new friend five.

What's that you say?

You only have five suction arms
And move at a pace of a slug.

Well, that's OK my little friend;
I'll just take a five arm hug!

The Flying Fish

While watching the sunset
In Puerto Vallarta,
With a rainbow in the sky,
A fantastic, fancy, flying fish
Soared into the sky.
She glided effortlessly
On the breeze.
Then gracefully she did descend
Into the sparkling emerald green sea.

Then she did it all again!

Precious

Precious was my little love bird.

She smelled so warm and sweet.

Her favorite food was millet sprays

Which she did daintily eat.

She would sit on my finger,

My head or my shoulder

At times she nibbled on my ear;

She would even let me hold her.

Precious was my little love bird

And now, she's truly free

And when I see her up in Heaven

I know she'll sing for me.

14

The Lovely Lime Colored Lizard

The lovely lime colored lizard
Scurried along the limb,
And even though he scurried very fast,
He saw us and we saw him.

He was such a handsome reptile;
We couldn't help but stare
In multiple shades of glistening green
His scales he did proudly wear.

Anaconda

Anaconda, anaconda
Oh so long
Cylindrical body
Rotund baton
Waiting and lurking
In rivers and in streams,
He's certain to devour
Whatever he deems.
Silent serpentine
On the steamy jungle floor
His coils are like a vice
His jaws a cold steel door.

Mobil SkyScraper

Mobil Skyscraper

Long, lanky and lean

Super slim Jim

That's Mr. Giraffe

On the scene

Snake like tongue

Prehensile to be exact

Rounding up some tasty leaves

For a noontime snack.

Jungle Life

Little monkey, little monkey

Cute, furry and brown

Picking mangoes and bananas

Before they hit the ground

Little frog, little frog

Sitting yellow and still

No one wants to eat you

'Cause your poison can kill!

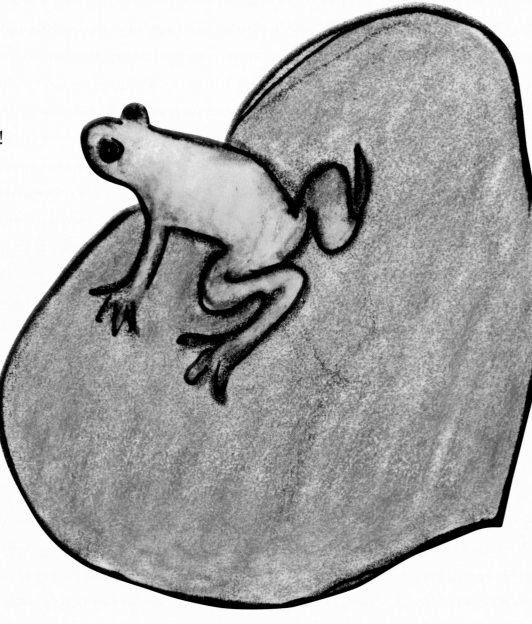

Little bird, little bird

Rainbow plumage in flight

Devouring hordes of bugs and mosquitoes

With all your might

Little tiger, little tiger

Golden and brown striped

Stalking prey with his brothers

In the steamy jungle night.

Rabbit

Hopping, nibbling

Soft, white and alert

Dining in Momma's vegetable garden

Then hiding under her skirt.

Conejo

Kitty

Stretching, purring

Soft, beautiful fur

Balancing gracefully along
the back yard fence

Feline

Puppy

Running, playing, tripping

Cuddly ball of fur

Licking my face

On the cheek

Canine

Bat

Black-webbed wings

Flying by sonar

Sleeping upside down in caves by day

Pollinating fruit trees by night

Rodent

Otter

Diving, clowning

Sleek, speedy swimmer

Dining on shellfish in the cove

Mammal